Environmental Awareness:
LAND POLLUTION

AUTHOR
Mary Ellen Snodgrass

EDITED BY
Jody James, Editorial Consultant
Janet Wolanin, Environmental Consultant

DESIGNED AND ILLUSTRATED BY
Vista III Design, Inc.

BANCROFT-SAGE PUBLISHING, INC.
601 Elkcam Circle, Suite C-7, P.O. Box 355
Marco, Florida 33969-0355

Library of Congress Cataloging-in-Publication Data

Snodgrass, Mary Ellen.
  Environmental awareness—land pollution / by Mary Ellen Snodgrass;
edited by Jody James, Editorial Consultant; Janet Wolanin,
Environmental Science Consultant; illustrated by Vista III Design.
    p. cm.—(Environmental awareness)
  Includes index.
  Summary: Details the various types of land pollution and possible
ways to prevent them.
  ISBN 0-944280-29-3
  1. Soil pollution—Juvenile literature. 2. Land use—Environmental
aspects—Juvenile literature. [1. Soil pollution. 2. Pollution.] I. James,
Jody, Wolanin, Janet. II. Vista III Design. III. Title. IV. Series: Snodgrass,
Mary Ellen. Environmental awareness.
TD878.S66   1991
363.73'96—dc20

**International Standard
Book Number:**
Library Binding 0-944280-23

**Library of Congress
Catalog Card Number:**
91-8303
CIP
AC

PHOTO CREDITS

COVER: Vista III Design; Craig Challgren p. 8; Nancy Ferguson p. 16, 32; J.E. Kirk
p. 10, 37; K.G. Melde p. 28; Silver Image, Mark Dolan p. 29, Richard Hobbs p. 12,
15; Minnesota PCA p. 35; Unicorn Photography, Rich Baker p. 7, Eric R. Berndt p.
38, Richard B. Dippold p. 26, Robert W. Ginn p. 22, Martin R. Jones p. 21, Martha
McBride p. 24, Aneal Vohra p. 41; Vista III Design, Ginger Gilderhus p. 25, 45,
Grant Gilderhus p. 4, 14, 18, 31, 40, 42, Jackie Larson p. 19.

MAR - - 2005

TABLE OF CONTENTS

We must maintain healthy soil to provide food for the people of the world.

CHAPTER ONE

THE IMPORTANCE OF LAND

The earth is our home. To maintain life, the earth must have healthy soil. The best soil contains a blend of water, air, minerals, and living things. These elements must exist in a balance.

If the balance is healthy, plant roots, earthworms, and digging animals will keep the soil loose and well blended. **Humus**, which is decaying matter that was once alive, serves as a sponge to soak up rain and help maintain a steady soil temperature. When this system works well, healthy soil serves as a kind of living filter for water, which helps keep the **environment** healthy.

Digging animals help keep the soil loose and well blended.

THREATS TO THE LAND

Unfortunately, much of the earth's environment is not in balance. All across the United States, people are discovering **pollution** on the land. Whether on farm land, mountains, beaches, parks, or back yards, citizens are realizing that the land is not as clean as it once was. Waste and chemicals from many sources create hazards for human and plant life. Because plants, people, and animals depend on the land, the increase in pollution is a serious matter for everyone.

Here is how the Weldons learned about the dangers of land pollution as they prepared to till the ground for a spring garden.

Pollution across our land has become a major problem.
Everyone must do their part to clean up our environment.

Digging in the soil, pulling weeds and watching plants grow in healthy soil can be a satisfying experience.

8

Marisa heard the bump of the wheelbarrow as her father rolled it across the brick walk. Another sound told her that he had opened the back of the station wagon and was loading his gardening tools. Nothing pleased Ted Weldon as much as digging a garden.

The Weldons shared a small patch of land at the edge of Claremont, Wyoming. Along with their neighbors, the Hudsons, they planted enough vegetables each year to fill their freezer. They even had some left over to share with others.

Marisa, who loved working in the garden, hurried out of bed and into her jeans. Like her father, she enjoyed digging in the soil, pulling weeds, and watching things grow. Best of all was her own row, where she planted marigold seeds, some spring onions, pumpkins, and a few shasta daisy plants.

By the time she got downstairs, her father had loaded the wheelbarrow, a shovel, and a hoe. Marisa hurried to see if she could help.

"What can I do, Dad?" she asked.

"How about putting your seed packets and a trowel into your mother's basket," he suggested. "And don't forget the gloves. I don't want you to get blisters again this year."

"Okay," she replied and ran off to the tool shed to help her mother with the last of the packing.

9

People who dump toxic waste on the land make it unusable for growing crops.

Soon the Weldons had everything packed in the car and were on their way out to the garden. They passed Green Lake and turned right onto the dirt road that led to the shared vegetable patch. Ted parked the car next to Jeff Hudson's pickup truck.

"Hey, Jeff! Are you all ready to start this season's tomatoes?" he called out cheerily to his neighbor.

Jeff looked sad and shook his head as he walked over to Ted's car. "It looks like we won't be gardening here ever again, Ted," he said.

Ted and his wife exchanged surprised looks. "Why, Jeff? What's happened?" Loretta Weldon asked.

"A county health inspector telephoned my office yesterday," Jeff replied. "He says that midnight dumpers have been polluting this area."

"What have they put on our garden?" Marisa asked as she leaned out the window for a better look.

"Well, Marisa," Jeff answered, "it seems they've emptied containers of dangerous chemicals from a factory in the next county."

"What kind of chemicals, Jeff?" Ted asked with real concern in his voice.

"The inspector said he found **PCB's**, lead paint, and **dioxin**. I don't know too much about the dangers, but I do know that those chemicals are bad stuff," said Jeff.

"They certainly are," agreed Loretta, who worked at a local laboratory as a chemical analyst. "PCB's can cause deformed babies. Lead can poison the body, and dioxin may cause **cancer**. We certainly don't want food grown in this soil."

As the Weldons said goodbye to Jeff and backed out on the road, Marisa felt like crying.

"Gosh, Dad, can't we grow anything this year — not even tomatoes?" she asked.

"Marisa," he replied, "we'll have to look for another plot of land where it is safer to plant our spring garden. Until we find one, we can plant our tomatoes in a pot on the patio."

"It doesn't seem fair," Marisa replied. "Why do people do such terrible things to the earth? Don't they know that dumping chemicals is dangerous?"

How can people allow land pollution such as this to accumulate?

CHAPTER TWO

THE LAND AND YOU

Marisa has asked some serious questions. Yes, most people know that dumping chemicals causes harm to the environment. Governments make laws that require businesses to handle dangerous materials with care. But there are people who pay no attention to these laws.

Do you agree with Marisa about the dangers of dumping chemicals on the land? Do you think land pollution is a serious problem? What reasons might people have for midnight dumping? Are there other forms of land pollution? How can citizens protect the land from pollutants? These and other questions about land pollution deserve careful thought.

From good, healthy soil come the useful minerals that make fruits and vegetables grow.

LAND AND POLLUTION

Land is an important part of nature. It provides a place for green plants to grow. From good, healthy soil come the useful minerals that make trees produce leaves and gardens grow vegetables and fruits. Animals and people depend on the health of soil for their own well-being. If soil becomes polluted, it passes along dangerous chemicals to the roots of plants. If these plants are used for food, the pollutants in them harm the bodies of humans and animals.

Pollution also affects the rain, dew, and melted snow that soaks into the ground. When polluted water seeps into rivers and streams, it poisons fish and animals. When polluted water kills plants, the soil beneath begins to **erode**. Without strong roots to bind the land, much of the **topsoil** washes away. The loss of topsoil into waterways chokes fish and plants that live in the water. The danger of pollutants spreads rapidly and can affect a whole community.

When polluted water seeps into rivers and streams, it poisons fish and animals.

*Chemical fertilizers applied to farm crops can
be another cause of land pollution.*

SOURCES OF POLLUTION

Where do these pollutants come from? The experience of Jeff Hudson and the Weldon family shows one serious source of pollution, deliberate dumping. Many factories and businesses make dangerous chemical wastes. For example, manufacturers of plastics produce PCB's. Paper factories use strong **bleaches** to whiten their products. Laboratories that make **antibiotics** and other useful drugs, also have problems disposing of deadly waste they produce.

Other serious pollutants include chemical sprays. When farmers, gardeners, and landscapers kill weeds with an **herbicide**, they put a deadly poison on the land. When they spray plants with an **insecticide** to kill Japanese beetles, grubworms, and other chewing insects, they endanger birds, small animals, frogs and toads. Helpful insects, such as bees and ladybugs are also destroyed. In addition, these chemical insecticides affect farm and orchard workers who handle the crops.

When cows, chickens, and other farm animals eat **contaminated** grass and grain, the poisons stay in their bodies. These poisons harm the people who drink their milk or eat their eggs and meat. For these reasons, chemicals used on farms and gardens can threaten the human body in many ways.

Chemical fertilizers, another cause of land pollution, may solve one problem and create another. They provide **nitrogen** to the soil and help plants to grow more rapidly. However, when the nitrogen **leaches** from the soil, it causes tremendous growth of **algae** and other simple green plants along creek banks and river bottoms. This growth clogs waterways, kills plant and animal life, and destroys the balance of nature.

Pollutants such as insecticides, herbicides, and fertilizers do not stay in fields, orchards, and lawns. Rain carries chemicals into **irrigation** ditches and streams. There the chemicals pollute drinking water as well as lakes and rivers. Soon these pollutants affect everybody, including swimmers and other people who fish and seek recreation.

People depend on laws to decide how the land will be kept healthy for growing vegetables and grains.

CHAPTER THREE

MAKING THE BEST USE OF OUR LAND

As citizens of one land, we must live together with many people. We must share the use of the earth with businesses, mines, hospitals, and factories. We also must depend on farmers and gardeners to provide food, shade trees, lawns, and flowers. Because different people have different uses for the land, there must be laws to decide how the land will be kept clean. We must have workers who check the soil for dangerous chemicals so that everyone can feel safe about using the land.

Nurseries are required to sell healthy plants to their customers for safe gardening.

WASTE DISPOSAL AND THE LAND

There are many reasons that some land is not safe. One of the most serious threats to the earth is the disposal of dangerous or **toxic wastes**. Some of the methods that people have used in past years are no longer considered effective.

City **dumps** have been a cause of much pollution. At one time, there were no rules about what items could be left in the dumps or how they could be disposed of. Water **runoff** carried pollutants from the dumps to nearby yards and farm land. These dumps are no longer allowed because they quickly become serious polluters of the land.

Other methods of waste disposal have not been effective. For a time, chemical plants and laboratories placed wastes in **sinkholes** and **injection wells**. By forcing pollutants into deep holes in the earth, workers at first believed that the materials could no longer cause harm. But modern studies of the earth have proved that these wastes do not remain in the holes. They pollute **ground water** and the **aquifers** from which people get their drinking water.

Another shortcut that people once used for waste disposal was dumping into the ocean. They believed that toxic waste and garbage in sealed barrels and bags would sink harmlessly to the bottom and remain there. However, containers do not always stay sealed.

Much waste washes up on shores and pollutes beaches. Some chemicals enter shellfish, such as oysters and clams. The shellfish then poison the people who eat them. For these reasons, officials decided that dumping wastes into the ocean was not good for the environment.

Water runoff carries pollutants from dumps to nearby streams and farm land.

Crowded cities create more demand for more goods.
More goods create more garbage which is threatening all life.

TOO MANY PEOPLE

A serious form of land pollution is caused by overcrowding in cities. When too many people live close together, they create more body wastes, garbage, and trash than can be safely disposed of. Often, **water treatment plants** and **sewage treatment plants** cannot remove harmful germs and other dangers fast enough or completely enough. When sewage treatment plants are flooded with rainwater, they sometimes overflow. The polluted water carries foul smells and disease to the land.

People cause another problem by constantly demanding more things. When people buy clothes, toys, appliances, magazines, and other goods, they create a need for more factories. More goods also create more garbage. In crowded cities, particularly on the east coast of the United States and in some places on the west coast, the problem of more factories and more garbage is threatening all life. The spread of factories takes up more land, leaving less for farming and recreation. The resulting wastes from the factories add to the problem of land pollution.

Crowded cities also need more hospitals and dental and medical services. Hospitals and doctors' offices create serious types of pollutants, such as used bandages, disposable needles, **amalgam fillings** for teeth, and **x-ray** supplies. If these pollutants are not kept away from the land, they can cause disease as well as **heavy metal** and **radiation poisoning.**

Vehicle exhaust is one of the most serious of all pollutants.

TOO MANY CARS

A serious source of land pollution comes from cars, trucks, buses, trains, and planes. Machines that burn **fossil fuels**, such as gasoline, oil, and jet and diesel fuels, pour out harmful fumes, especially **sulfur dioxide** and **carbon monoxide**. These pollutants fill the air and settle back on the land.

When fossil fuel pollutants are mixed with moisture in the air, they return to earth as **acid rain**. This strong rain eats away rubber, metals, cloth, marble, and other building materials. But more important, it soaks the land and throws off the balance of useful chemicals in the soil.

An additional problem with cars is that they require batteries, tires, antifreeze, and **lubricants**. These materials create disposal problems. Old batteries can pollute the land with sulfuric acid and heavy metals, such as nickel, cadmium, lead, and mercury. The burning of old tires and the disposal of antifreeze and oils also create land pollution. With more people driving each year, the problem is growing fast and needs immediate solutions.

When fossil fuel pollutants mix with moisture in the air they return to Earth as acid rain. This strong rain can scar and destroy buildings.

CAUTION

CONTAINS

PCBs

(Polychlorinated Biphenyls)

A toxic environmental contaminant requiring
special handling and disposal in accordance with
U.S. Environmental Protection Agency Regulations
40 CFR 761--For Disposal Information contact
the nearest U.S. E.P.A. Office.

In case of accident or spill, call toll free the U.S.
Coast Guard National Response Center:
800:424-8802

This sign indicates toxic waste danger from PCBs in the transformers. Special handling and disposal of this waste is regulated by the Environmental Protection Agency.

CHAPTER FOUR

CLEANING THE LAND

Once soil is polluted with pesticides, chemical fertilizers, trash, sewage, fuel exhaust, and toxic wastes, it is difficult to clean. In some areas polluted by PCB's and dioxin, sanitation workers dig up the soil, place it in barrels, and take it to storage sites carved in rock deep in the ground.

Other types of pollution can also be treated. For example, acid soil from acid rain can be treated with lime. The lime process returns to normal the chemical balance in the soil and makes farm land and yards more suitable for growing healthy plants.

Unfortunately, not all polluted land is easily cleaned. Because the work is dangerous to workers and the cost is high, the **Environmental Protection Agency (EPA)** sometimes closes polluted land to public use. In New York State, chemical dumping ruined a whole neighborhood called Love Canal. Instead of cleaning up the pollutants, the agents kept people from coming in contact with the dangerous material. This method meant, however, that people had to abandon their homes. The neighborhood was too polluted for families to live in.

Since no cleanup method is easy or cheap, officials advise people not to pollute. By suggesting ways of avoiding land pollution, these advisers help keep people free of the diseases and birth defects caused by dangerous wastes.

PREVENTING MORE POLLUTION

An early improvement in controlling land pollution was the creation of **sanitary landfills**. These areas replaced dumps as gathering spots for garbage. Sanitary landfills are lined with heavy clay or plastic and are filled with layers of waste topped with layers of soil. These added liners protect the soil underneath from any dangerous liquids.

Heavy earth-moving machines gradually fill in the landfill and pack it down to create a solid base. When the landfill is full, a final thick layer of soil hides all trace of garbage. The land then can be reused for parks, playgrounds, schools, or homes.

Several other methods of managing waste help keep the ground free of pollution. One method is waste **reduction**. To reduce the amount of dangerous waste, workers separate and remove safe materials. Then the dangerous materials take up less space. Because the dangerous wastes are now smaller, they are less trouble to pack and carry away. They can be stored in barrels so as not to pollute the land.

Sanitary landfills are one method of controlling land pollution.

Heavy earth-moving machines fill in the landfill and pack it down to create a solid base.

Heat and flame are two more methods of reducing toxic waste. Some hospitals heat harmful waste, such as human tissue and infected blood, in special **microwave** ovens. A second method used on hospital wastes is **incineration,** which reduces the wastes to ash. By heating or burning these pollutants, hospital workers keep harmful bacteria from entering the soil through landfills and spreading infection.

Factory owners can use another method of disposing of dangerous waste. The owners can pour pollutants into **lagoons.** These artificial lakes have plastic linings to prevent soil pollution. To remove dangerous pollutants from the lagoons, the owners add organisms to eat and digest the pollutants. When the material is no longer dangerous, it can then flow through sewage pipes into ordinary treatment plants.

To keep **strip mining** from ruining soil, laws prevent owners from bulldozing and piling up **slag,** which is a **by-product** of mining operations. These laws also limit the amount of acid that mine owners can drain from mines. To rebuild the land, some mine owners **backfill** holes in the earth with healthy soil.

To replace the green plants that the heavy equipment removed, farmers and foresters replant the areas around mines with trees and grass. By improving the health of the soil, the farmers and foresters return it to productive use for crops or animal **habitats.** Farmers also encourage the use of **microorganisms.** These tiny living cells break down dead leaves, branches, and other **biodegradable** matter that falls on the land.

Farmers and foresters replant the area around mines with grass and trees.
By improving the health of the soil the land can be returned to productive use.

If more people used mass transit the land would be
less polluted by fossil fuels.

REDUCING POLLUTION FROM CARS

Cars are even worse for the land than factories, hospitals, and strip mining. Since the late 1960s, government agencies have enacted laws to help control exhaust. For instance, new cars, buses, and trucks cannot be sold without **catalytic converters**, which are devices that change harmful gases into safer exhaust. These converters raise the price of new vehicles as well as the cost of vehicle operation. At the same time, they help control pollution that fills the air and falls back on the land.

Some laws help reduce pollution by requiring the removal of lead from fuel. Lead, like mercury, zinc, and arsenic, is a dangerous heavy metal. When it enters the lungs, it can poison the body. Lead poisoning can cause severe problems to the brain. Because lead poisoning is so deadly, laws require people to buy gasoline that is lead-free.

Highway planners help reduce pollution by keeping traffic moving. When traffic moves smoothly and evenly through intersections, cars spend less time standing still with the motor running. A better design for traffic reduces the amount of exhaust that pollutes the soil.

A great help to stopping pollution from cars would be a change in fuel. If drivers could easily find a clean, cheap fuel, they could help solve the problem of pollution. One possible fuel is a form of alcohol made from corn or sugar cane. A switch from fossil fuels to alcohol would also give farmers a new market for their crop.

An even greater solution would be less dependence on cars for transportation. In many cities, a single person drives to work or school in a car. If more people shared rides, took the bus or subway, rode bicycles, or walked, the land would be less polluted by fossil fuel fumes. The promotion of new forms of **mass transit**, such as bullet trains or elevated people movers, would further reduce the number of cars on the road. This improvement would keep the land cleaner.

MAKING SAFER FACTORIES

Factories and power plants, just like cars, must burn fuels to operate. Because large factories use great amounts of coal, gas, and other raw materials each day, they produce tons of polluted gases. One of the most unpleasant of these gases results from the **sulfur** that is found in coal. When it forms hydrogen sulfide, it gives off a smell like rotten eggs. When it forms sulfur dioxide, it becomes a poisonous gas.

Some of these gases can be made harmless by the addition of water or chemicals. Others, however, are directed into the air as smoke through smokestacks. According to clean air laws, smokestacks must be taller than the surrounding buildings or hills. From this height, the smoke rises above where people live and work. As long as the smoke stays high in the sky, it is less likely to pollute the land. In addition, to halt heavy particles or **fly ash**, factory owners cover smokestacks with caps that trap solids and keep them from falling back on the surrounding land. Then the factory owners dispose of the ash in sanitary landfills.

More up-to-date devices help cut down the number of particles that escape. Some smokestacks are equipped with a **flare tip** to reduce land pollution. This device injects steam into the gas as it leaves the smokestack. The addition of steam helps reduce the amount of smoke by making the gas particles too heavy to escape up the smokestack. Sometimes the steam can eliminate pollutants entirely.

Another air pollution control device magnetizes the waste particles. The particles stick together like magnets and fall harmlessly out of the way of escaping smoke. Later, factory workers gather the particles and dispose of them safely in sanitary landfills.

Factories that have **recovery systems** actually vacuum the gas as it escapes. These systems cool the hot gas, remove valuable chemicals, and collect them in barrels. Then the factories reuse the chemicals. Such systems not only cut down on land pollution, but also save expenses.

Factories and power plants produce tons of polluted gases each day.

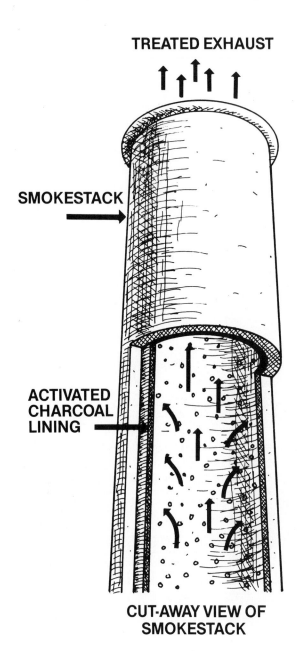

TREATED EXHAUST

↑ ↑ ↑ ↑ ↑

SMOKESTACK ➤

ACTIVATED CHARCOAL LINING ➤

CUT-AWAY VIEW OF SMOKESTACK

Many harmful particles can be trapped by lining the upper section of the flue with activated charcoal.

Some smokestacks contain **scrubbers,** which are devices that remove the harmful particles from factory exhaust. These devices help make smokestacks even more effective. By lining the upper section of the **flue** with **activated charcoal,** factory owners can trap most of the harmful particles and change them into safer by-products.

Another method of reducing factory pollutants is to control raw materials. When factory owners substitute less harmful solids, liquids, and gases, they cause fewer pollutants. In this way, factory owners cause less land pollution. By showing concern for the land, the owners become good neighbors to the people who live close to their buildings.

DOING YOUR PART

Everyone has a role in keeping the land clean. The Environmental Protection Agency (EPA) is a government agency that takes charge of pollution problems. The EPA tries to protect people and the environment. This agency keeps a close eye on ash from factories and incinerators. It also examines drums filled with toxic and radioactive wastes. It measures heavy metals and harmful chemicals in the soil.

The Environmental Protection Agency examines drums filled with toxic and radioactive wastes.

Do your part by recycling at school and work. Many goods can be reused rather than dumped where they can pollute the soil.

CHAPTER FIVE

THE INDIVIDUAL'S PART

The average person cannot stop land pollution singlehandedly. However, each person can decrease activities that cause dangerous particles and fumes to pollute the land. Marisa Weldon studied land pollution at her local library. Here is a list of suggestions she put together to help prevent pollution. Her suggestions are the kind that anyone can do.

PROTECT THE SOIL

1. For short distances, travel on foot or by bus, mass transit, or bicycle. If you must go by car, combine several errands in one trip.
2. Start a **carpool** in your area. Share rides to school and community activities. Shop with a friend or neighbor.
3. Keep vehicles in good condition by having frequent engine tune-ups. A clean engine burns fuel more efficiently.
4. Consider alternate fuels for vehicles, such as propane, methane, ethanol, or corn alcohol.
5. Burn only dry hardwoods in fireplaces. Avoid using the fireplace or woodstove as a garbage incinerator. Keep chimneys clean.
6. Never dump fireplace ash on soil if the ash contains heavy metals or other pollutants from burned magazines or metallic wrap.
7. Establish containers for recycling aluminum cans, glass, plastic, paper, and cardboard. Make frequent trips to a recycling center so that these goods can be reused rather than dumped where they may pollute the soil.
8. Read labels to be sure that products are not harmful to the environment.

To avoid herbicides and insecticides, pull or hoe weeds.

40

PROTECT YOURSELF

1. Never pick berries, mushrooms, or other edible plants along a highway or near a factory where pollution or pesticide and herbicide sprays may have coated them.
2. Create a **compost** heap to recycle grass clippings, leaves, and kitchen wastes. Mix the compost with lime and soil and turn it frequently. When the compost changes into a usable soil builder, add it to gardens and flower beds.
3. To avoid herbicides and insecticides, pull or hoe weeds; spray insects with insecticidal soap.
4. Study science to help you understand the complex materials that pollute the earth.
5. Dispose of used paint cans, batteries, and other toxic materials according to local, state, or federal laws. Avoid dumping or burning anything that may cause land pollution.
6. Ask questions. Read articles about pollution. Study ways of making healthy soil. By learning more, you can be an effective voice against land pollution.

Dispose of used paint cans or anything toxic according to local, state or federal laws.

ENCOURAGE GOVERNMENT OFFICIALS TO TAKE ACTION

1. Write or call local officials or state or national representatives. Encourage them to vote for stronger anti-pollution laws.
2. Support citizen's groups, such as those that police factories, power plants, airports, and strip mining operations. Insist on heavy fines for polluters.
3. Observe the soil in your area. If you see evidence of pollutants from factories, call a representative of the Environmental Protection Agency near you.
4. Support laws that require drivers to use lead-free fuel and catalytic converters in their vehicles.

ENCOURAGE INDUSTRY TO KEEP THE EARTH CLEAN

1. Avoid products made by manufacturers who pollute or who refuse to cooperate in the clean up and protection of the soil. Also avoid products that are covered by too much wrapping, especially cellophane, aluminum foil, and other non-recyclable materials.
2. Write thank-you notes to companies that are making an effort to keep the earth clean.

Do your part to protect the environment. Report land pollution such as this to your local officials.

GLOSSARY

acid rain (A syd RAYN)   rain or snow that mixes with sulfur dioxide and nitrogen oxide and is more acidic than normal

activated charcoal (AK tih vay tihd CHAHR kohl)   carbon grains that filter impurities from the air

algae (AL jee)   simple one-celled green plants that grow in water

amalgam fillings (uh MAHL guhm FIHL ihngz)   mixtures of mercury and silver used to fill cavities in teeth

antibiotics (an tih by AHT ihks)   drugs made from microorganisms to kill other microorganisms

aquifers (A kwih fuhrz)   places under the earth where water collects

backfill (BAK fihl)   to fill a hole with the original soil taken from it

biodegradable (by oh dih GRAYD uh buhl)   capable of breaking down into harmless by-products

bleaches (BLEECH ihz)   chemicals that whiten

by-product (BY prahd uhkt)   a waste product made by a factory while it is creating useful goods

cancer (KAN suhr)   a disease in which human body cells grow abnormally

carbon monoxide (KAHR buhn muhn AHK syd)   a deadly, odorless gas that results from car exhaust and the incomplete burning of fossil fuels

carpool (KAHR pool)   sharing of rides

catalytic converters (kat uh LIHT ihk kuhn VURHT uhrz) devices in cars that make exhaust less harmful

compost (KAHM pohst)   dead leaves and other decaying plant material

contaminated (kuhn TAM ih nay tihd)   anything that is polluted

dioxin (dy AHK sihn)   a dangerous chemical found in herbicides

dumps (DUHMPS)   places where garbage is left out in the open

environment (ihn VYRN mihnt)   anything that influences life and makes living possible

Environmental Protection Agency (EPA)   a federal agency that helps protect the environment in the United States

erode (ee ROHD)   wash away

flare tip (FLAR TIHP)   a device in a smokestack that helps stop particles from escaping by mixing them with steam

fly ash (FLY ASH)   solid particles of dust, soot, and ash that are carried away from a fire by air currents

flue (FLOO)   a tube in a chimney, through which smoke is drawn off

fossil fuels (FAHS ihl FYOOLZ)   fuels that come from decaying plants and animals under the earth; oil, coal, and natural gas are fossil fuels

ground water (GROWND wat uhr)   water that collects below the earth's surface

habitats (HAB ihtats)   places where an animal or plant lives and grows

heavy metal (HEHV ee MEHT uhl)   metals, including zinc, mercury, lead, chromium, and arsenic, which can poison humans and animals

herbicide (UHRB ih syd)   chemicals that kill plants

humus (HYOO muhs)   decaying plant and animal matter in soil

incineration (ihn sihn uh RAY shuhn)   burning in special concrete ovens

injection wells (ihn JEHK shuhn WEHLZ)   deep holes which are drilled in the rock beneath the earth and filled with waste material

insecticide (ihn SEHK tih syd)   a chemical that kills insects

irrigation (ihr ih GAY shuhn)   a system for watering plants

lagoons (luh GOONZ)   artificial lakes

leaches (LEECH ihz)   wash out or dissolve

lubricants (LOO brih kuhnts)   oil and other liquids that help machine parts move smoothly

mass transit (MAS TRANS iht)   ways of travel, such as buses and subways, which carry many people at one time

microorganisms (my kroh OHR guhn ihzmz)   tiny one-celled animals and plants

microwave (MY kroh wayv)   a method of heating using short electronic rays

nitrogen (NY troh jihn)   a substance necessary for plant and animal life

PCB's   industrial pollutants that poison animal tissue

pollution (puh LOO shuhn)   dirtying of natural resources

radiation poisoning (ray dee AY shuhn POY zuhn ihng) destruction of body tissue from contact with too many x-rays or other radioactive forms of energy

recovery systems (ree KUHV ree SIHS tuhmz)   devices that take chemicals out of the air and return them to storage for later use

reduction (ree DUHK shuhn)   a way to decrease the amount of dangerous waste by removing harmless particles

runoff (RUHN ahf)   soil particles that are carried downhill by rain or melting snow

sanitary landfills (SAN ih tar ee LAND fihlz)   areas where garbage is safely buried away from water supplies

scrubbers (SKRUHB uhrz)   devices in smokestacks that collect harmful particles and prevent them from dirtying the air

sewage treatment plants (SOO uhj TREET mehnt PLANTZ) a place where household waste water is cleaned before it's released back into the environment

sinkholes (SINK hohlz)   natural depressions in the earth where water collects

slag (SLAG)   a waste by-product of mining

strip mining (STRIHP MYN ihng)   a mining operation that strips away the soil that covers a valuable mineral such as coal

sulfur (SUHL fuhr)   a chemical found in coal

sulfur dioxide (SUHL fuhr dy AHK syd)   an air pollutant created when gasoline is burned in cars and coal is burned in power plants

topsoil (TAHP soyl)   soil at the surface of the earth that contains humus and nutrients for plant growth

toxic wastes (TAHK sihk WAYSTS)   wastes which can poison living things

water treatment plants (WAHT uhr TREET mihnt PLANTZ) a place where water is cleaned before it is piped to homes

x-ray (EKS ray)   strong particles or beams of energy used in medical treatments